Original title:
Life's Puzzle: I Lost the Box

Copyright © 2025 Creative Arts Management OÜ
All rights reserved.

Author: Alexander Thornton
ISBN HARDBACK: 978-1-80566-242-6
ISBN PAPERBACK: 978-1-80566-537-3

The Map without a Legend

In a land where paths just twist and twirl,
I follow signs that swirl and swirl.
With arrows pointing everywhere,
I wonder if they even care!

A treasure map, or just a prank?
I find a tree, they call it 'Blank.'
Three steps forward, then two to the side,
Is this the way to the chocolate guide?

An Odyssey in the Void

In a ship made of cardboard, I set sail,
With a captain's hat and a big bag of ale.
The stars above are made of cheese,
I'm lost for words and blissfully pleased.

Is that a whale or just my friend?
The joke of the night will never end.
Oceans of milk, I float with glee,
Turns out the treasure's just a big cup of tea!

Threads of Disarray

I knitted a sweater, or was it a kite?
With colors that clash, a true fashion fright.
My yarn unraveled in the blink of an eye,
Now I'm dressed like a sad, lost pie.

The patterns get tangled, no end in sight,
Each stitch is a battle, a comical fight.
"Wear it with pride!" my cat seems to say,
I guess I'm just trendy in a wobbly way.

Patches of Uncertainty

I fixed the carpet with scraps that I found,
Now it looks like a circus turned upside down.
With polka dots here and stripes over there,
My guests now arrive with a chuckle and stare.

The couch is a beast with cushions askew,
You sit down with caution, it might swallow you.
Here's a quilt with a story no one can tell,
Perfect for dreams of nonsense—oh well!

The Fractured Arrangement

In the corner, pieces lay,
Some look happy, others stray.
A dog chewed one, now it's gone,
Matching colors? That's withdrawn.

A cat sits on the missing square,
Winks at me, like she don't care.
I try to fit them, upside down,
Is this a puzzle or a clown?

Unraveled Directions

The map is ripped, the edges torn,
Where's the part that I was sworn?
Instructions vague, they might confuse,
Think it's a puzzle or my muse?

My fingers fumble, slipping fast,
A jigsaw dance, what a contrast!
Those pieces laugh, they like the tease,
Maybe they just want some cheese?

Pieces Scattered by the Wind

Out in the yard, a piece took flight,
Twirled and spun in pure delight.
The neighbor's cat gave chase with glee,
But that piece? It's just too free.

I chase it down, but force too hard,
Fell on my face, now that's retarded!
The jigsaw pieces giggle near,
Maybe this tug-of-war's sincere?

Echoes of a Hidden Assembly

In the attic, echoes ring,
Of missing bits, and lost bling.
I heard a laugh; was it my mind?
Or just these shapes that tease and bind?

The tweezers, scissors, all in hand,
But all they do is jest and stand.
Each corner's edge just mocks my heart,
In this assembly, where to start?

A Jigsaw of Memories

Pieces scattered wide, so bright,
Laughing at my morning fright.
Where's the corner, where's the edge?
Is this a game, or a soggy hedge?

Coffee spills on a photo spree,
Was that a cat or a bumblebee?
Shapes and sizes, can't decide,
Is this a challenge, or a silly ride?

Lost in thoughts, I twist and twirl,
Trying to fit in this jigsaw swirl.
Grandma's face looks quite askew,
Did she wear that hat—oh wait, it's blue?

Searching frantic for that one piece,
It's under the couch, like a naughty lease.
With a grin, I declare my win,
Who knew chaos could ever begin?

Unraveled Threads

Tangled yarns in a messy heap,
Where did I put my threads to keep?
Socks without matches, oh what fun,
A knitting war I've surely won!

Stitch by stitch, my mishap grows,
Is that a sweater or just clothes?
A scarf that's short, a muffin top,
I laugh so hard, I just might flop.

Grand designs turned into clucks,
Where's my needle? Oh, bad luck!
Unraveled hopes from yesterday,
Yet here I sit, not far away.

In every knot, humor found,
Each tug a giggle, love unbound.
A world in threads, all intertwined,
In this wild chaos, peace defined.

The Colors of Absence

Grab a brush, oh what a sight,
Colors splattered, pure delight.
Where's the canvas? Who can say?
This magical mess, a bright ballet!

Red for joy, green for the sly,
But where's that blue I thought I'd buy?
A rainbow absent, life misplaced,
Yet laughter here can't be erased.

Splashes and drips, I dance around,
Each vibrant hue, a silly sound.
Artistic chaos, my cherished foe,
Where's the box? I'd like to know!

In colors lost, I paint my cheer,
In shades of happy, bold and clear.
From empty frames, a chuckle spills,
Absence thrives where laughter fills.

Disjointed Whispers

Muffled secrets float in my head,
A puzzle that was once well-read.
Words that wander, thoughts dismayed,
It's like a circus that won't be swayed.

Chatter here and laughter there,
I swear this game isn't really fair.
Did I say that? Oh, what a mix,
Disjointed lines, I've lost my fix.

A pun here, a joke misplaced,
Trying to keep up, I match the haste.
With every slip, I find more glee,
This laugh-out-loud catastrophe!

Swirling whispers, humor reigns,
In this hodgepodge, joy remains.
Once a puzzle, now a spree,
Embracing chaos will set me free!

A Mosaic of Wistfulness

Pieces scattered all around,
A cat is chasing, what a sound!
Mirrors reflect a troubled face,
Jigsaw dreams in a crazy race.

Coffee stains on the old floor,
Forgotten keys and socks galore.
Humpty Dumpty on the wall,
Had a great fall, and that's not all.

A picture frame that's upside down,
Worn-out shoes, a missing crown.
Searching high, searching low,
Where's that piece? I just don't know!

Chuckling at the grand old mess,
Each lost bit tells me, "Do not stress."
In this chaos, memories dance,
Life's a giggle, given a chance.

Riddles in the Ashes

Once a puzzle, full of flair,
Now it's smoke, hangs in the air.
Pieces burnt, but jokes remain,
Riddles hidden in the mundane.

A crooked frame without its queen,
Ghosts of patterns rarely seen.
Pencil marks on a crumpled sheet,
Sketches of life, comic and sweet.

Playful whispers from the past,
Frivolous laughs, they always last.
The pieces laughed from their repose,
Tickled me pink as laughter grows.

Finding shapes in what was lost,
Turns out it's a fun-filled cost.
Ashes to ashes, but what a sight—
Each riddle making life more bright!

Chasing Vanished Shapes

Shapes elude like shadows flee,
Running wild, quite differently.
A circle dances with a square,
    Frantic chases fill the air.

Tangled strings of thought and play,
They giggle softly, wax and fray.
Trying to catch a fleeting grin,
Until I trip—it's fun to spin!

Squares wear hats and triangles sing,
The clutter hums with everything.
A race against the clock's own hand,
Chasing shapes that sink like sand.

Finding joy in silly spins,
Drowning sorrows where laughter begins.
Each vanished shape teaches me,
To enjoy the chase and be carefree!

A Symphony of Silence

In quiet corners, whispers play,
Missing pieces laugh away.
Cacophony of silent calls,
Echoing through empty halls.

The sock sings a strange old tune,
While waiting for the afternoon.
A symphony of lost old things,
In every pause, the laughter rings.

A key that fits in all the wrongs,
Unlocks the heart where humor throngs.
The tablecloth waves a merry greeting,
In a dance of silence, retreating.

Chasing echoes, nothing's clear,
Finding joy far and near.
In the stillness, giggles hum,
A silent orchestra, beats of fun.

Portrait of a Broken Design

I tried to piece the bits I found,
But one was a shoe, the other a hound.
A jigsaw nightmare, I must confess,
These shapes don't fit, oh what a mess!

The corner is missing, the edges are curled,
My artwork's a joke to the entire world.
I laugh with the chaos, paint splattered bright,
In this broken design, I find pure delight.

Time's Discarded Shapes

Clock hands are wobbly, they tick wrong,
Each hour's a giggle, the chime's a song.
Seconds slip sideways, as time takes a twist,
A rubbery moment, it's quite hard to miss.

With circles that wobble and squares that bend,
These shapes were meant to play, not to end.
I wave at the minutes, as they dance out of line,
In this silly conundrum, I sip my cold wine.

A Canvas of Forgotten Forms

Colors collide like a wild daydream,
Some splattered like ketchup, others like cream.
An octagon's laughing with a triangle's grin,
While rectangles whisper, 'Where do we fit in?'

I spin the brush, oh what a scheme,
On this canvas, nothing's as it seems.
Brush strokes make monsters, and swirls start to hum,
In this joyful chaos, I know I'll have fun.

Glimpse of the Unseen Whole

Peeking at pieces all over the floor,
Finding a puzzle I never signed for.
A cat with a hat and a fish on a chair,
I wink at the madness, without any care.

Together they giggle, a bizarre little crew,
A circus of shapes spilling out like goo.
In this hodgepodge of nonsense, I let laughter roll,
I found joy in the fragments, my funny little whole.

Embracing the Unknown

I tried to fit a cat in a hat,
But it just ran off, imagine that!
My socks have found new places to roam,
Yet somehow, I still feel at home.

The fridge sings songs of previous guests,
While I decode these culinary tests.
The remote is a ghost, forever lost,
Still, my attempts come at no real cost.

My keys play hide and seek with my head,
Perhaps they just want to stay in bed.
I dance with chaos, a wacky partner,
Inventing new steps, a spiral charmer.

With every twist, a smile appears,
As I embrace my scattered fears.
The ride is bumpy, but oh so bright,
In this circus of odd, I find delight.

Shadows in the Corner

In the corner, shadows sneak and laugh,
Dancing away like they've had a giraffe.
I question my sanity more than once,
Wondering if they're just pulling a stunt.

Dust bunnies host their own grand ball,
While I'm tracing patterns on the wall.
Every creak echoes a pitter-patter,
As I search for the source of the chatter.

Invisible friends with peculiar traits,
Rescue me from my lone dinner plates.
With a wink, they declare, "Let's have a feast!"
And serve me a dish of pure nonsense, at least.

In this house, where whimsy takes hold,
My treasure map's scribbles are gold.
For every shadow lends wisdom to me,
Nonsense becomes sweet symphony.

Scattered Moments

Today I lost a shoe on the stair,
Where could it be? I wouldn't dare!
My coffee's gone rogue, spilled with flair,
Seems fate has tagged it – just don't care!

A spoon plays tag with my cereal bowl,
As time drips slowly, my daily toll.
With cereal rainbows filling my heart,
I chuckle at where every piece plays its part.

Yesterday's plans went fizzling away,
Yet giggles linger, come what may.
I gather the moments, like lost pennies,
Trading them for laughter, oh so many!

For every mishap turns to silly gold,
Stories to tell when we're gray and old.
These bits and pieces, I don't want to mend,
In this wild ride, I've found a friend.

The Art of Reconstruction

With mismatched furniture on display,
I'm building a fortress in my own way.
Frames minus pictures, just stylish air,
Facing the chaos, I dance without care.

Meanwhile, my plans are a jigsaw tease,
Last seen at a barbecue by the breeze.
They float like balloons and vanish, oh dear,
Yet laughter erupts as the end draws near.

I'm an architect of dreams gone astray,
Constructing fun castles, come seize the day!
Each wall represents my quirky delight,
Where every rumor turns wrong into right.

So I'll mix and match, make a mess with pride,
Embrace every odd turn and whimsical ride.
In this art of reconstruction I'll see,
The beauty found in my jumbled esprit.

Whispers in the Interstitial

In the corner of my mind, bits collide,
A mismatched sock, my thoughts can't hide.
Where did I place that missing piece?
I search and search, but I can't find peace.

A cat that darts, a dog that prance,
They seem to know the secret dance.
I spill my coffee, sighs in the air,
Is this a riddle or an old affair?

Giggles echo from the pantry door,
I swear I heard it—was it just folklore?
Dancing spoons and forks that tease me,
A banquet of chaos, oh where's the key?

Yet here I am, a grin so wide,
Embracing the fun, with fluff as my guide.
Tangles I weave with colorful thread,
In this circus of life, I'll dance instead.

Chasing an Elusive Picture

The snapshot fades, edges worn,
I chase a blur, a tale reborn.
Where is the laughter that framed the day?
In the clamor of chaos, it slipped away.

Mismatched memories, a jigsaw grand,
The edges don't fit, it's hilariously bland.
A treasure map with no 'X' in sight,
Just a rubber chicken—what a delight!

I pose with pillows, a goofy grin,
As if capturing joy is my ultimate win.
Filters and flashes, but nothing is real,
I find myself laughing at the oddest appeal.

Yet in the hunt, I find my song,
In jumbled laughter, I truly belong.
Every mistake a brushstroke fine,
In this artwork of whimsy, my heart will shine.

Threads of Woven Memories

Yarn strewn about, a colorful mess,
I tug at a thread, in playful jest.
Balloons drift high, a squirrel runs by,
Where's the recipe for my last pie?

Grandma's old quilt with patches so bright,
Holds secrets of times lost to night.
I trip on the hem, land flat on my face,
Is this the fabric of my silly race?

Each tangle a story, each knot a cheer,
I laugh at the days gone, year after year.
In a tapestry woven with threads of delight,
I find joy in the chaos, a twinkling sight.

So here's to the weavings of mismatched charms,
The wayward threads that keep me from harm.
In every misstep, I stumble, I grow,
With laughter my pattern, I dance in the flow.

The Absent Cornerstone

In the depths of my thoughts, a block is awry,
I search for the cornerstone, oh me, oh my!
Building my dreams on a sandy ground,
With laughter and bubbles, I spin all around.

The architect's plan—a pot full of beans,
Blueprints of whimsy, all in my dreams.
I hammer away at a muffin so round,
What's this construction? It's upside-down!

I shuffle the pieces, a game of charades,
Each box I open, a new escapade.
A garden of giggles, weeds growing high,
But I pluck at the roots and let laughter fly.

So while my foundation may seem quite absurd,
I've built my own castle where giggles are stirred.
With cracks full of joy and walls made of cheer,
Let's toast to the madness, my dear, never fear!

Remnants of What Could Have Been

A sock here, a shoe over there,
Where's the partner? I just don't care!
The puzzle snapped; pieces all scattered,
Trying to find them, it really doesn't matter.

The chicken crossed, but lost its way,
Searching for eggs at the end of the day.
In the chaos of colors, nothing is neat,
I'll grill 'em up, and make a fine treat.

My keys are lost, in a Bermuda hallway,
Under cushions where they like to play.
A sandwich, I swear, is lurking around,
In the depths of my bag; it makes no sound.

Yet, laughter echoes through this disarray,
In the mess, there's joy, come what may.
A good chuckle is worth all the fuss,
Who needs the box? Let's just make a plus!

Tapestry of Unraveled Threads

Once a ball of yarn, now just a chase,
Knots and tangles make a funny face.
Cats love my chaos, with little regard,
While I tug at threads, it's just so hard.

A needle's point, with missing eye,
Sews together tales that seem to fly.
With mismatched socks and absent gloves,
I find my solace in warmth and shrugs.

What if I lost that scissor blade,
And the snacks are always a trade?
With jellybeans and dreams, I will thread,
A tapestry vibrant, where silly is fed.

So I laugh as I knit my strange delight,
In this crazy quilt of a fractured night.
No perfect seams, just giggles abound,
In my threadbare art, true joy is found!

Song of the Unassembled Pieces

Oh, the joy of parts that never align,
A jigsaw dance of the oddest design.
With corners and edges, they mock me with glee,
Like a rock band full of cats sipping tea.

A lid with no pot, what a strange affair,
Rolling on floors with no hint of a care.
My chairs they wobble, my table is proud,
The sight of this madness, I can't help but crowd.

And the broken clock chimes at the wrong time,
A chorus of chimes, all out of their rhyme.
Hiccups ensue, as I puzzle and play,
In this comedy of errors, let's frolic away.

Together we twirl, in this offbeat song,
Singing of chaos, where we all belong.
An orchestra strange, but we revel in cheer,
For the pieces unite, when laughter is near!

The Journey Beyond Edges

Once a smooth path, now bumpy and wild,
Adventure awaits, like a curious child.
With bags full of wonders, I set out to roam,
In a world full of whimsy, I've built my own home.

The coffee spills fast in this wobbly car,
As I navigate lives, like a shooting star.
I stop for some snacks, all strewn in a heap,
The mess of my travels sends me into deep sleep.

Maps without routes, are better for fun,
Lost in the moments, oh, how I've run!
With a smile on my face, I chase after dreams,
In this journey of edges, nothing's as it seems.

So laugh as we wander through thickets and trees,
With each twist and turn, let's savor the breeze.
The path may be crooked, but joy is the prize,
In this grand escapade, let's rethink the skies!

Conversations with the Void

I spoke to the empty chair,
It winked with a bright flair.
"Where's the puzzle?" I did ask,
It chuckled, hiding behind a flask.

The cat just yawned with glee,
As I searched under the tree.
"Do you know where it's been?"
It purred, all cozy and keen.

I checked my old coat, it was bare,
The void just giggled, unaware.
"You won't find it here, my friend,"
The chair replied, "It's just pretend!"

So I danced with shadows in delight,
The void, my partner in the night.
We twirled amidst lost things,
And laughed at the chaos that life brings.

The Quest for Unifying Elements

In the kitchen, I made a mess,
Hoping to find some success.
Flour flew like a wild dream,
As I searched for a missing seam.

The toaster ignored my plight,
While the fridge laughed with delight.
"Maybe it's in the cupboard high?"
The pan replied with a sigh.

I ventured to look at the yard,
Where squirrels carried puzzles hard.
"Have you seen my missing piece?"
They danced away, laughing with ease.

I spilled my coffee with a grin,
Perhaps the hunt for fun begins.
And in the chaos, I found a clue,
That laughter is the best glue too!

Clarity in the Smudge

I drew a picture, oh so grand,
With colors not quite planned.
The smudge became my best friend,
As it twisted in a playful bend.

"Is this a cat?" I asked in jest,
The smudge responded, "I'm the best!"
"You're messy!" I said with a laugh,
It grinned, saying, "I'm your other half!"

Paint splattered on the wall,
While I tried to not let it fall.
"Where's the sense in all this?"
The smudge grinned, "In joyful bliss!"

We created chaos, oh so bright,
In every corner of the light.
With my smudged friend, I can't complain,
For every blunder brings its gain!

Tangents of a Hidden Journey

I took a wrong turn at the moon,
And danced to an offbeat tune.
A rabbit offered me his hat,
Saying, "That's not where the fun is at!"

I chased shadows around the block,
Where every clock tried to mock.
"Is this where my piece resides?"
The duck quacked while he glides.

Around the bend, a goat stood tall,
Asking if I'd seen it at all.
"You are lost but oh so found,"
He winked and turned around.

So I wandered with a chuckle clear,
Embracing each bump without fear.
In the midst of all that I roam,
I learned that joy's where I call home!

Words Between the Spaces

In a world of missing parts,
I find a sock that plays its arts.
Puzzles take a sip of tea,
While I chase the cat up a tree.

Lost the lid that fits my pan,
And I can't recall the plan.
With every twist, a giggle breaks,
As the pie crust dances, oh, what mistakes!

Under the couch, I spy a clue,
A stray remote, is it mine or new?
The fridge hums a happy tune,
As I search for lunch in the afternoon.

Oh where's that piece that fits just right?
The one that sparkles, a pure delight.
I toss the shapes and have some fun,
Life's silly chaos has just begun!

The Search for Familiarity in Absence

Forgotten keys make a quiet sound,
While laundry piles up, round and round.
The clock ticks on but I stand still,
Hunting lost treasures, oh what a thrill!

A sandwich waits on a counter high,
With mustard dreams, it asks me why.
The fridge sings songs of yesterday,
As I ponder what to eat today.

Echoes of laughter skip through the air,
While memories dance without a care.
A wink from a friend, a knock on the door,
Each moment feels like a quirky encore.

With mismatched socks, I strut my stuff,
The world's a stage, it's all just fluff.
Finding the joy in what's amiss,
Turns out this search is pure bliss!

Kaleidoscope of Unsung Journeys

I took a trip down a winding lane,
Only to find my shoes were in vain.
A map that leads to nowhere fast,
Hilarity strikes, this is a blast!

I bumped into a tree with a grin,
"Guess I'm home!" it said with a spin.
With breadcrumbs scattered by brave little birds,
I forge ahead, despite the absurd!

Each twist and turn, a joyful plight,
A raccoon steals snacks, what a sight!
With laughter echoing through my head,
I dance with the stars instead of dread.

So here's to journeys that make no sense,
Finding true joy through the nonsense.
In a world where paths twist and twine,
The unexpected is truly divine!

Symphony of the Unfinished

My to-do list is a melody sweet,
With chorus lines that can't find their beat.
I start to write but lose my pen,
Ah, the song of 'Oops!' begins again!

Dishes piled like unplayed notes,
Each one sings and subtly gloats.
With a broom as my baton, I conduct,
A symphony of chores that seems obstructed.

The socks in shadows start to dance,
While I plead for just one more chance.
Each half-finished task, a quirky verse,
In the grand opera of this universe.

So I embrace the chaos, let it play,
For there's humor in the mess we display.
With laughter ringing through the halls,
This symphony of unfinished calls!

Revisiting the Void

In the closet, I found a shoe,
Where did you go? It's just one, boo!
Socks are missing, a mystery so grand,
In my house, the lost items band.

My keys keep dancing, avoid my grip,
Do they have plans for a road trip?
A whimsical search, for the sake of fun,
I'll gather the lost—just one by one.

Jigsaw pieces under my bed,
A puzzle that's lost, or so it's said.
Maybe they're partying, I'll join the craze,
Who knew a floor could host such displays?

With random bits scattered around,
There's joy in the chaos that I have found.
A misplaced life, but oh so spry,
Let's embrace the mess, just let it fly!

Embracing the Unfinished Story

A book half read, with pages bent,
Where did I leave off? I can't lament.
A plot twist hiding, behind a chair,
Maybe the cat knows, with her stare.

I'll write my tale, with fragments bright,
Like scattered stars in a comical night.
Characters missing, they lost their way,
But that's the fun in this wild essay.

The plot coils like spaghetti on a fork,
Twists and turns, a playful quirk.
My mind's a scribe with coffee and dreams,
The laughter echoes in silly memes.

Each sentence starts, yet ends in flair,
Who needs a finish when you have an air?
An unfinished story, let it roam free,
In the world of chaos, it's a lovely spree!

The Echo of Lost Connections

I called my friend, but got a cat,
What do I do with a furry diplomat?
Can I borrow whiskers, for a laugh?
His sly purrs seem to edit my path.

The dial tone giggles, a pause in scream,
Lost connections aren't as they seem.
Each missed call a note in this tune,
A soundtrack crafted by a clumsy moon.

I text a ghost, with emojis bright,
In this digital ether, lost in light.
But maybe they'll answer, just on a whim,
In the echo chamber, I'll dance with him.

With each lost link, I squeeze a grin,
What a wild ride, let's begin!
Lost connections transform the real,
Into funny tales that make us feel!

Landscapes of Disjointed Journeys

A map with scribbles, hard to decode,
Where's my destination? I've lost the road.
It's a scenic view, with giggles and sighs,
As I wander aimless under blue skies.

With a compass spinning like a crazy top,
Every step forward feels like a flop.
But in these tangents, I find my stride,
The joy of detours takes me for a ride.

Funky landscapes of jumbled delight,
Each misstep a dance in the shimmering light.
Through the valleys of chaos, laughter abounds,
In this mixed-up realm, joy knows no bounds.

So here's to journeys with no real goal,
And the beauty found in an unscripted scroll.
With a heart full of giggles, let's play this part,
In this wild adventure, let chaos be art!

The Heartbeat of Lost Pieces

In my bag, there's a sock,
A keyring, a half-eaten rock.
Buttons scattered like tiny stars,
Their origins lost in memoirs.

The cat's got my thumbscrew now,
It's king of the missing, wow!
A paperclip wedged in my shoe,
What else is hiding? A llama too?

A tangle of strings, oh what a sight,
From my last birthday's ill-fated flight.
The treasure map's been so well used,
I think I'll just claim I've been confused.

Who needs maps when I've got a mess?
Features of chaos, I must confess.
A life so vibrant, like confetti rain,
Each piece a laugh, none fit the same.

Searching for the Unseen Boundary

I searched the fridge for my missing ear,
Found a mayonnaise jar wearing a sneer.
Oregano sprouted a funny face,
What once was salad is now a space.

The remote control's taken its stand,
In the couch's deep, mysterious land.
No chip, no dip, all crumbs in my sight,
Swallowed in cushions, perhaps out of spite.

Maps crumbled at my flimsy grasp,
Each trail leads to a memory clasp.
To wander aimlessly, oh what fun,
Finding boundaries that never were won.

So here I am, in the chaos I roam,
A traveler lost, but I'm still at home.
With laughter and whimsy in every step,
In a world where I chose to inept.

The Invisible Stamp of Time

Days drift by like socks in the wash,
One's on the floor, the other's posh.
Calendar's marking an invisible race,
Every wrinkle a time stamp, just add some grace.

The clock's hands spin in a comical dance,
Tick-tock confetti, give it a chance!
Here lies a spoon, a fork on the ground,
Where did my sense of direction rebound?

The fridge is a bank for my lost cheese,
Moldy regrets, oh how they tease.
A sandwich sent to an uncharted shore,
I guess I'll eat cereal; who can ask for more?

As moments dissolve with a cheery grin,
I laugh at the chaos that swirls within.
For time's just a puzzle, not meant to adjust,
In the haze of reasons we never discussed.

Landscapes of the Disintegrated

In my garden, weeds sprout like dreams,
Each one a puzzle, or so it seems.
The gnomes have snuggled into the dirt,
Wearing cobweb hats, and not a hint of hurt.

The grass whispers secrets, tickling my feet,
Sandwiches hidden where locusts meet.
Every flower a chapter, each bud a tale,
Bees buzzing loudly, what's in the mail?

The horizon has vanished with socks left behind,
Torn bits of fabric, the cosmos unlined.
I swear I planted a charming grapevine,
Now it's just weeds with a smidge of sunshine.

Let's toast to the messes still waiting to bloom,
With laughter, bright colors, and an untidy room.
For in my odd garden, joy clearly thrives,
In landscapes of chaos, oh how it jives!

Pieces of a Forgotten Dream

I once had a dream with a jigsaw twist,
But pieces were missing, oh what a list!
I found a few chickens and a shoe with a lace,
Now I'm building a chicken house, just in case.

One edge looked like pizza, quite hard to believe,
And a corner was shaped like a leaf of a weave.
I laughed as I sorted through scattered delight,
The more that I searched, the funnier the sight.

At times I would ponder, what fit where and when,
As a cat played the role of my crafty friend.
Chasing down pieces that ran from my hand,
This puzzle of laughter was merely unplanned.

So here sits my dream with no box to be found,
Just a quirky assortment that's quite spellbound.
Each piece tells a story, however bizarre,
In this jolly old game of "Where the heck are?"

Shattered Reflections

My mirror cracked silly, its image a joke,
With faces and creatures that giggled and spoke.
One half had a duck with a top hat so grand,
While the other just showed me a strange piece of sand.

I tried to piece together the laughter and cheer,
But shadows danced wildly, not one seemed sincere.
Paint splashed like madness across what once was,
In this wacky reflection, I didn't know who was.

A turtle performed a tap dance on air,
While the fish wore a cloak, so debonair.
With each broken shard, a giggle would flow,
This folly of mirrors just stole the whole show.

So I'll share with the world this fractured delight,
Where laughter's the glue and the colors are bright.
In the bits of the past where silliness reigns,
My shattered reflections have loosened my chains.

The Missing Edge

One day I was musing, my puzzle was bare,
With edges missing, it just wasn't fair.
I searched high and low, under socks and old hats,
Found a spoon and a turtle, but no edges, just chat!

The dog had a piece, I'm sure it was true,
He boasted of treasures and swallowed my shoe.
I patted his tummy, he wiggled with glee,
His grin was a riddle, 'Not my fault,' said he!

Two corners look grumpy while one is quite sly,
Each time I connect them, they whisper and cry.
"Where's the last edge?" I ponder and sigh,
Hoping it's not sailing the seas up high.

Yet in this mad scramble of missing for fun,
I cherish the chaos, I'm not quite done!
With humor in hand, I dive and dig deep,
In the wild where my puzzle pieces play hide-and-seek!

Fragments of Yesterday

I found a small paper, a cryptic old note,
With fragments of memories all scribbled afloat.
There's a penguin in slippers, a cat wearing ties,
And a fish on a bicycle, under bright sunny skies.

With bits of old photos tucked under the bed,
There's a goat with a backpack and a bird that just said,
"Why gather your pieces? Just let them run wild!"
As if fragments of yesterday were so beguiled.

I tossed out the rules, much to my surprise,
Laughter erupted as I opened my eyes.
No need for the box or a plan that's too tight,
This patchwork of nonsense was pure, unbound light.

So I'll stack up the fragments, make joy my own,
Each piece tells a story, each stitch overthrown.
In this whimsical world, where nonsense can thrive,
My fragments of yesterday are joyful, alive!

Finding Wholeness in Fragments

I searched for a piece beneath the couch,
Found a crumb from a snack, oh what a slouch.
The dog eyed me with a curious stare,
As if to say, 'Your life's quite a scare!'

Jigsaw pieces hide in strange places,
Under my bed, in odd little spaces.
Orange socks here, a shoe there,
But I'm still missing my favorite chair!

A button from nowhere lands on the floor,
Next to the toy that I used to abhor.
Collecting these bits brings a smile bright,
Creating a laugh from chaos and plight.

So here's to the scattered, the lost, and the stray,
Turning mishaps in a whimsical way.
With each little find, I dance with delight,
Making my mess feel just perfectly right.

The Language of Dispersed Shapes

What's this I see, a triangle near?
A piece from a game that once sparked cheer.
In the drawer of socks it decided to hide,
I chuckle alone, what a goofy ride!

Circles are rolling, they sway and they spin,
I keep finding shapes I forgot were in.
Each twist and turn, a laugh comes alive,
In this circus of shapes, I somehow thrive.

Squares are cornered, feeling so blue,
But they giggle when I show them what's new.
The language of chaos speaks loud and clear,
Every odd shape brings joy, that's for sure!

I gather these forms like a silly collector,
No need for an art team or even a mentor.
In this language of shapes, let's all have fun,
Building a world, one giggle, one pun!

Secrets in the Missing Pieces

Oh where did I put that secret of mine?
A puzzle piece lost just a rocks' throw from shine.
I peek in the fridge and look under the mat,
Finding leftovers, avoiding my cat.

A sock with a hole, how can that be?
It used to be grand, now a mystery.
My treasure hunt leads to a treasure map,
Filled with lost items and a cereal trap!

I ponder the secrets of all that's been gone,
Like a magician's act with a curious con.
Each missing piece tells a silly old tale,
Of missing cookies and unusual mail.

Let's celebrate joy in what we can't find,
Turning lost bits into laughing unwind.
In every odd corner, a secret can grow,
As I dance with the fragments, in a vibrant show!

The Dance of Disconnected Lives

On the floor, a solo socks' dance starts,
A left foot lost in amusing parts.
They twirl and they whirl, with freedom unmatched,
In the realm of mismatches, joy is dispatched.

I once knew a spoon that knew quite a tale,
It pranced with a fork, but they ended up pale.
Together they laughed, like old friends in line,
In a messy kitchen, they breathed life divine.

The shoes excitedly hop on a spree,
In mismatched pairs, they feel so free.
Each step's a delight, a jumble of cheer,
In the dance of the disconnected, no one shows fear.

So here's to the laughter that chaos can bring,
In the dance of our fragments, let's all shake and sting.
For together we make a most beautiful sound,
In quirky connections, our joy can be found!

Fragments of Who We Were

Once upon a time, we strolled,
With mismatched socks and dreams untold.
A map in hand, but no clear way,
We laughed at what the lost might say.

With puzzle pieces, we'd create,
A wiggly frame—oh, isn't fate great?
We played with colors, bold and bright,
Yet some parts just never felt right.

We'd search for faces in the crowd,
But each one seemed to wear a shroud.
The key was lost, the door ajar,
We hummed along to a wacky guitar.

So here we are, in twists profound,
Collecting odd bits we've found.
For in the gaps of our strange lore,
We share a giggle and look for more.

The Enigma of Unattached Edges

Puzzles lie scattered, oh what a mess,
Corners are missing, can you guess?
The cat stole a piece and hid it away,
While I pondered life—what a game to play!

Edges unknown are now my fate,
I'll fit them in, or just contemplate.
Cracks and curves, don't you fret,
These fine mismatches are my new pet.

Each piece a chuckle, a joke unseen,
A dance of whimsy, a twist of trim.
Who needs the box, with maps unclear?
I'll embrace the chaos, let's bring the cheer!

So here's the truth, as wild as can be,
Missing the box has set me free.
In unattached edges, I find delight,
With laughter brightening every night.

A Symphony of Broken Images

A jigsaw symphony sounds quite grand,
With notes of nonsense, hand in hand.
Each piece calls out, "Is this my friend?"
As I ponder on how they might blend.

A cat on a piano brings a smile,
As notes scatter wide, just for a while.
The trumpet's missing, replaced by a shoe,
Can you hear the melodies that we brew?

The orchestra shrieks, the colors collide,
Fractured shapes in a joyful ride.
In this wild concert, laughter's the theme,
We create a tune that bubbles with steam.

So if you find fragments, don't be dismayed,
Let music guide you, don't be afraid.
For in the chaos, joy shall arise,
A broken song that never says goodbyes.

The Search for Completion

With a puzzled frown, I search the floor,
For missing bits I can't ignore.
Like socks in a dryer, they tend to hide,
I embark on a quest, I'm filled with pride.

"Here, piece here!" I call with glee,
As my dog runs off with a part from me.
A scavenger hunt, so curious and fun,
In the realm of confusion, we've just begun.

Each inquiry brings laughter, each clue a smile,
Gathering fragments, a whimsical style.
I'll sew them together, a tapestry bright,
With threads of humor, it feels so right.

So let's keep searching, oh what a game!
For in the chase, we'll stake our claim.
Completion's a jest, but joy will ensue,
In every odd piece, I find the you.

A Journey Beyond the Frame

Up in the attic, I found a tray,
Pieces of colors, all mixed in a fray.
The corner looks blue, but there's a bright red,
Is this a puzzle or just my morning bread?

Lost in the corner, I spot a small cat,
Sitting on pieces, he's wearing my hat.
Is he a helper, or just a sly thief?
I laugh as he guards my puzzle of grief!

With each tiny fragment, I dance and I grin,
Life's just a game, let the chaos begin!
Finding the corner, a piece looks surreal,
Is that a dragon, or just my last meal?

With laughter and joy, I search for the clues,
In a world so silly, there's nothing to lose.
When nothing fits right, I giggle and sigh,
Maybe the answer is simply to fly!

Fragments of an Unfinished Jigsaw

A thousand bits scattered across the floor,
Shaped like a dance, or maybe a door.
I pick one up, it's a half-eaten pie,
Is that my dinner, or just a plain lie?

The edges are missing, my patience runs thin,
I swear I had pieces to give it a spin.
A sock from last winter sneaks under my heel,
Is this part of the puzzle? Oh, what a surreal deal!

A fish and a slipper seem lost in the maze,
Where's the picture? I'm caught in a haze.
With giggles and grunts, my fingers connect,
As laughable shapes take on lives to reflect.

In this wild mess, I stumble and glide,
Each piece I encounter unveils the absurd side.
I'm crafting a creature with six legs and a nose,
If that's not a puzzle, I don't know what goes!

Shadows of Missing Pieces

In the corner, a shadow, a shape that looks wild,
Is it a puzzle or my inner child?
A piece that seems to smile, a piece that seems blue,
Who knew my puzzle had a sense of the true?

With laughter that echoes, I plug in a spot,
It fits like my grandma's old polka dot.
This cat's on the table, my coffee's on him,
Is he solving my jigsaw, or just feeling grim?

A duck with a hat perched high on a hill,
Do ducks wear hats? Oh, what a thrill!
The pieces keep dancing, like stars in a groove,
Maybe in chaos, we all start to move.

Oh, how I wonder what treasure lies near,
In a world full of laughter, there's nothing to fear.
Missing a few, but I'll call it my art,
In this puzzle of shadows, it's a laugh from the heart!

The Puzzle's Silent Echo

Echoes of laughter swirling in air,
A stray little piece hiding under my chair.
What was the picture? A bird or a bee?
I guess it's a buffet for the curious me!

With each bright fragment, I spin and I twirl,
A castle of laughter begins to unfurl.
A pair of mismatched socks joins in the fun,
Together we puzzle until we're all done!

The cat's got a scheme, or perhaps just a snack,
One paw holds a piece while the other's off track.
I burst out in giggles, my puzzle is shy,
Behind every corner, is a wink and a sigh.

In the quiet a chuckle, a joyful refrain,
This puzzle I cherish is hard to explain.
As pieces elude me, I search and I grin,
In laughter's sweet chaos, is where I begin!

Stitched Together in Silence

In a room full of quirks, I fix my seams,
Sewing thoughts of nonsense, crafting dreams.
A button misplaced, a zipper gone wild,
I laugh at the chaos, the heart of a child.

A sock on my hand, a hat on my foot,
I twirl in confusion, oh what a hoot!
With fabric and laughter, I dance on the floor,
Each stitch tells a joke, who needs a chore?

The needle's my sidekick, the thread is my friend,
In this wacky adventure, there's no need to mend.
So I'll keep on sewing this tale of delight,
In silence we giggle, from morning to night.

With a quilt of my quirks, I snuggle up tight,
Surrounded by stitches, it all feels just right.
In this funny fabric, I patch up my frown,
For a world full of laughter, I'll never back down.

Chaos of Unmatched Edges

Pieces on the table, all colors and shapes,
A puzzle of life where laughter escapes.
No corner to start, no edges in sight,
Just random confetti, what a silly plight!

A blue piece with yellow, a red in the mix,
I fumble and giggle, trying out tricks.
This chaos is funny, it tickles my brain,
Like searching for rainbows while dancing in the rain.

The cat thinks it's playtime, pouncing around,
I lose all my pieces, they scatter the ground.
But who needs a box when the fun's in the chase?
I cherish this madness, a smile on my face.

So here in the mayhem, with joy I declare,
These mismatched edges are treasures to share.
With laughter as glue and time as my guide,
I'll cherish each piece, let humor abide.

Searching for the Frayed Thread

A spool of mischief, a tangle of cheer,
Searching for threads that just seem to disappear.
Tug at the knots, oh what a surprise,
My fabric of folly, a truth in disguise.

One thread leads to nowhere, another goes wild,
With yarn balls of laughter, I'm still just a child.
A fray here, a pull there, oh what will I find?
In the mess of creation, I'm humor entwined.

A knitting disaster, a pattern askew,
But who needs perfection when joy's come to view?
With stitches of giggles and loops made of fun,
I'll unravel the madness until I'm all done.

So here is my mission, my colorful quest,
To gather the fragments, I must give my best.
In a tapestry woven with laughter and dread,
I'll celebrate all the threads, both lost and widespread.

A Map Without Coordinates

I opened the atlas, what a sight to behold,
A map drawn in crayons, adventures untold.
No north, south or east, just streets made of play,
Where giggles and sunshine brighten the way.

I wander the pathways, a treasure I seek,
With dragons and unicorns perched on their peak.
Each page is a riddle, each line is a test,
Exploring this world, I'm laughing the best.

With x's and o's, I scribble my route,
In the land of confusion, I spin round about.
But who needs directions when joy's my GPS?
I'll chart out my journey, no need for success.

So I'll blaze my own trail, through laughter and cheer,
No map will define me, my path is quite clear.
With each twist and turn, I embrace all my woes,
For the journey is funny, wherever it goes.

A Diary of Altered Directions

I woke up one day, with socks mismatched,
A grand adventure planned, but the map was scratched.
My coffee spilt right on my shoes,
But hey, there's always room for snooze!

I tried to find my keys, oh what a joke,
Tossed in the fridge with some leftover smoke.
I asked the cat for advice, so wise,
She blinked and then claimed her prize!

The GPS led me to a cornfield trail,
I met some chickens, had an epic fail.
I told them my dreams of finding home,
They clucked and agreed—they'd never roam!

At day's end, I sat with a grin so wide,
The wild journey felt like quite the ride.
So misplaced, yes, but never lost,
With a heart full of laughter, I count the cost.

Building Castles in the Air

In a kingdom where clouds build up high,
I crafted a tower, my dreams learn to fly.
With marshmallow bricks and a jellybean roof,
I called to the squirrels, 'Come check out my goof!'

They gathered around, with acorns in hand,
To judge my creation, they formed a grand band.
But as they sang, the whole structure did sway,
One large sneeze, and it all blew away!

With laughter they scattered, not one left behind,
While I chased after candies that fluttered, so blind.
A song for the winds, I did also compose,
To cheer up my spirits when all goes to blows!

No blueprints were needed—just whimsy, my guide,
In the sky, I'll find joy, where magic resides.
For what good's a blueprint, when dreams can transpire,
By building with laughter, I reach even higher.

The Imprint of Unfolding Mysteries

A box at the door, wrapped up with a bow,
I opened it wide, but a tangle did flow.
Out came the socks, that should've been pairs,
I laughed till I cried, with clothes everywhere!

From paper and tape, a rabbit did hop,
Then danced out a toaster, a thick-buttered flop.
I wondered allowed, 'What else can I find?'
A wild kazoo? I'm losing my mind!

The secrets I uncover, one giggle at a time,
Unraveling items without any rhyme.
With each wacky find, I let out a cheer,
For this silly chaos, brings everyone near!

So here's to the mysteries, hidden in boxes,
Where laughter erupts, and we all lose our socks.
With wonder and joy that spills out like wine,
In the oddities unveiled, our hearts align.

Dreaming of a Unified Canvas

With colors in jars, splattered on a wall,
My paintbrush went dancing, a free-for-all.
I dreamed of a canvas, painted with glee,
But ended up rainbowing my cat and me!

The dog joined the party, in a splash-and-play,
He rolled in the hues, made the mural sway.
With paw prints of teal and a tail of bright red,
Our masterpiece barks while the kitty fled!

Neighbors popped in, peeking through the hole,
"Is this abstract expression, or total console?"
With laughter and chaos, they picked up a brush,
In this vibrant mess, we felt quite the rush!

So here's to the days when art takes a twist,
Where unified chaos is too good to miss.
For who needs perfection in colors and lines,
When laughter is painted in fun, without signs!

Reflections on the Disarray

A sock went missing, where could it be?
My shoe's dating hat, looks quite silly,
The fridge hums a tune of discontent,
While spoons and forks have their own fun bent.

I found a puzzle piece, under the couch,
Its shape looks like a squashed-out grouch,
The cat claims pieces like a trophy war,
I guess she's winning, while I'm on the floor.

The clock ticks backward just to confuse,
Every left sock seems to join the blues,
My thoughts scatter like leaves in the park,
And laughter gets lost in a clattering lark.

In this jumble, we find our cheer,
Misplaced items bring joy, that's clear,
Embracing chaos, a dance on the floor,
Who needs a box? I've got plenty more!

The Harmony of Disconnected Notes

Spoons serenade forks in the drawer,
While a wayward lid rolls out to explore,
The banjo strums in an odd major key,
As potatoes join in, wild as can be.

The socks form a band, two left and a right,
Playing tunes that go bump in the night,
In the spaghetti pot, a waltzing noodle,
Says, "This is better than any old poodle!"

I've got a rubber band holding a dream,
But it snapped, sending wishes upstream,
A jigsaw missing, but it calls out with glee,
"Find me a match, where could I be?"

In this symphony of mismatched delight,
We embrace the quirks, what a sight!
A chorus of flukes taking center stage,
In the crazy concert, we're all the rage!

In Search of Celestial Order

Stars in the sky are a cosmic array,
But my utensils prefer a cabaret,
The moon spins tales to a teapot so round,
While galaxies giggle at the chaos they've found.

A thousand marbles roll down the stairs,
They whirl and twirl without any cares,
I'll catch them all with a butterfly net,
But they dance right away—what a silly duet!

The constellations point but they lead me astray,
A lost Tupperware, where'd it play?
The sun winks at me from its high throne,
While mismatched socks dance, feeling right at home.

In this universe, what's truly absurd,
The simple distractions are what I've heard,
A sprinkle of laughter in what feels off-track,
A joyful scramble, I won't look back!

When Pieces Refuse to Fit

A puzzle awaits, but pieces are few,
And a cat sits smug on what I pursue,
The corners are chewy, the middle bizarre,
While the picture's still hanging, up by the bar.

I've got two bird legs, but a whale in my hand,
And the ice cream carton thinks it can stand,
Each piece stubbornly wears its own hat,
Laughing at rules, what a curious spat!

The edges are rough, and the colors clash,
A game of patience, a merry old bash,
"Why fit," they yell, "when we can just play?"
As the world's puzzle stays lost, come what may.

So here we all are, a quirky brigade,
Creating our own little plans on parade,
No box to contain this whimsical show,
Just pieces that wander and roam to and fro!

Uncharted Territory

In a world of mismatched socks,
I wander through the cluttered blocks.
With puzzles missing, I just can't find,
The pieces meant to ease my mind.

A missing lid, a broken spoon,
Without the guide, I'm lost as noon.
I chuckle at how it never fits,
As laughter comes from all my flits.

The Enigma of Solitude

I sat alone with jigsaw dreams,
A cat beside me, plotting schemes.
He stole my pieces, one by one,
As I laughed, what's lost is fun!

With crumbs of snacks and coffee stains,
I build my world with silly gains.
Each missing part turns into jest,
My solitude, at least, is blessed.

Whispers of the Forgotten

Beneath the couch, the dust bunnies play,
While I search for pieces of yesterday.
Whispers echo—'You'll never find,'
Yet here I am, lost and maligned.

I find a button, a paperclip,
And chuckle at my wandering trip.
With every thought, a giggle ensues,
And in this mess, I'm happily confused.

Tapestry of Regrets

My tapestry is threads of haze,
Each stitch a tale of funny ways.
I skipped a beat, I missed a turn,
In all this chaos, still I learn.

With mismatched colors, I weave and tie,
What should be lost, I tell it, 'Why?'
And in the end, with a wink, I find,
The box was just a trick of the mind.

When Shadows Create

In the park, I lost my hat,
A squirrel claimed it, imagine that!
We danced around, he took a spin,
Guess my head needs extra tin!

My shoes got stuck in a muddy plot,
Wiggled my toes, oh what a knot!
The ducks just laughed, they are so sly,
Guess I'll need wings, oh me, oh my!

Clouds above, they hide and seek,
Whispering secrets, they're so cheek!
I chased a shadow, it made a run,
Turns out it's just the evening sun!

With every step, new tales unfold,
The world's a jester, bright and bold.
Losing my way is quite the fun,
Never a dull moment, just begun!

Boundaries of the Unattainable

I reached for cookies on the shelf,
Yet dropped the jar, oh dear self!
Crumbs and giggles all around,
My cookie monster turned profound!

The cat, she watches with a grin,
As my dance of fate begins to spin.
I tried to reach my dreams, you see,
But they flew off, just like a bee!

A trampoline seemed a smart affair,
But gravity said, 'You're still in air.'
Bouncing high, oh what a thrill,
Till I landed on my neighbor's grill!

So here I stand, with tales to share,
Embracing chaos with all my flair.
Boundaries tossed, with laughter and cheer,
Swinging between the absurd and sincere!

Searching for Footprints in Sand

At the beach, I lost my phone,
It danced away, all on its own.
Footprints shift with every tide,
Where did that pesky gadget hide?

I dug around with frantic zeal,
Found only shells and a big wheel.
The crabs applauded, what a show!
My treasure hunt was quite the go!

Seagulls squawked with tales untold,
They seemed to know, oh so bold!
Yet all I got was sandy toes,
And a midday sun that brightly glows!

As rays danced down and time did wane,
I left, still searching—a funny game.
Yet in the chatter of waves and sand,
I found joy in the chaos, unplanned!

The Weight of Untold Stories

A suitcase packed with tales galore,
I couldn't lift it, oh what a chore!
Stories of socks and jammed-up zips,
Lost in a whirl of misfit trips.

Each zipper locked like secrets tight,
Exploding laughter, oh what a sight!
From clumsy falls to pancake flips,
The weight of humor in each little quip!

I opened it once, a clown popped out,
With colorful pies and laughter about.
The neighbors gasped, what a ruckus then,
All part of my untold tales again!

So here I stand, with zany pride,
A burden lighter, what a wild ride!
The weight of stories is quite absurd,
In every mishap, there's joy inferred!

A Canvas Unfinished

Colors splashed without a thought,
Lines that swirl, yet mean a lot.
A brush in hand, the hues a mess,
I laugh aloud, who would have guessed?

Shapes that twist and giggle play,
A whimsical dance in bright array.
The masterpiece is lost in cheer,
Where's the box? Oh, it's not here!

What's a painter without a plan?
Just a jester with a crayon.
A canvas now is quite the sight,
As I draw cats that fly at night.

So here I paint, and here I dream,
With every stroke, a silly theme.
My art, a laugh, a gentle tease,
Creating joy, if you please!

What Lies Beneath the Surface

I dug a hole with giddy glee,
What might I find? A treasure spree!
A shoe, a sock, a rusty key,
And oh, the dirt—it tickles me!

Beneath the grass, it's quite absurd,
A collection of things, all quite blurred.
A button here, a toy that squeaks,
Digging deeper, laughter peaks.

I thought I'd find a pot of gold,
Instead, a story yet untold.
With every scoop, a burst of laughter,
What lies beneath? Just silly banter.

So if you dig, don't seek a prize,
Embrace the silliness that lies.
For in the muck, we find delight,
In every chuckle, there's pure light!

Echoes of a Broken Map

A map in hand, I squint and stare,
An X marked wrong, I wander bare.
With every turn, I lose my way,
Is that a landmark? Or just a ray?

Bumps and giggles, oh what fun,
A stroll with friends, all on the run.
"Is this the spot?" I ask with flair,
"We've found a bench, but treasure? Where?"

So off we go, on paths unknown,
Each twist and turn, a tale well sown.
With laughter loud, we roam the land,
No treasure chest, but happy band.

Maps can twist, but joy won't fade,
In every wrong turn, memories made.
So here's to roads that lead to smiles,
Forget the box, let's walk for miles!

The Heart's Missing Piece

A jigsaw heart, one piece askew,
With edges sharp, and colors too.
I laugh each time I try to fit,
Love is wild, and oh so split!

A corner here, a side that's gone,
A puzzle game, I laugh along.
With every turn of hope and cheer,
My heart's a riddle, loud and clear.

I mix and match with giddy love,
A piece that flies, like a dove.
Each missing slot a giggle brings,
Confusion reigns, oh how it sings!

Yet in this mess, I find my way,
In every gap, it's all okay.
For love's a game, so full of fun,
Let's dance together, one heart—one!

Colors Beyond Recognition

Once I had a rainbow, bright and bold,
But it slipped away, like stories untold.
Now I mix blue with yellow, quite a sight,
Drawing smirks from friends, oh, what a delight!

I tried to paint the grass, it turned out pink,
A color so weird, it made me rethink.
Should I laugh or cry at my vibrant dread?
Perhaps I'll start a trend, just forge ahead!

The clouds look fluffy, like cotton candy,
Yet nature giggles at this twist so dandy.
I skipped the brush, just used my hands,
Now my walls are art, where chaos stands!

In a world of color, I've lost the way,
Missing the box that held shades at bay.
But at least there's laughter while paints collide,
Every splash a journey, nowhere to hide!

The Art of Missing Links

Once a jigsaw puzzle sat pristine and neat,
I lost the corner piece, oh what a feat!
Now I'm left with gaps, a hodgepodge view,
A masterpiece born from the box that flew!

I tried to find logic in the random bits,
A cat, a shoe, and some strange little kits.
They tell me it's art if I just squint right,
But I still feel puzzled, not quite polite!

My friends drop by with their sharp questions,
"Where's the picture?" they search for suggestions.
I chuckle and shrug, it's all in the fun,
Who needs the box when we've already begun?

Each piece is a laugh, a tale to inspect,
Missing links connect in ways that reflect.
So here's to the chaos, the fun in the strange,
For life's wild jigsaw, I won't ever change!

Filling the Gaps with Dreams

In a garden of thought, weeds start to grow,
I forgot to plant seeds, oh no, woe is me!
Dreams tumble around like leaves in the breeze,
A colorful mess, but it's laughably free!

With gaps to fill, I sprinkle some cheer,
Imaginary daisies bloom, far and near.
I put on a crown made of daydream delight,
In this garden of whimsy, twirls take flight!

The sun's lost its bearings, it shines out of place,
Yet giggles emerge with the warmth on my face.
Who needs order when chaos feels right?
Let's dance in the shadows, embrace the odd light!

Dreams grow wild where the rules can't go,
My garden of laughter is all I bestow.
So here's to the gaps, let's toast them and cheer,
For filling with dreams takes away all the fear!

The Mysterious Edge of Existence

On the edge of existence, I wandered one day,
A signpost was broken, leading astray.
"Do not enter!" it read, with a quirky grin,
So I walked right through, let the fun begin!

The view was bizarre, a curious scene,
Penguins in tuxedos, what could it mean?
They stomped with flair, arguing about hats,
I couldn't help giggling at the silly spats!

In this limbo of nonsense, I found my crew,
Eccentrics galore, just a motley few.
A jester with dreams of a pie in the sky,
And a circus of clouds that simply float by!

So here's to the edges where logic takes flight,
In a world full of laughter, everything feels right.
We lose the box with its straight-laced confines,
And dance on the edge, where the whimsy shines!

Constellations of Missing Stars

In the sky there's a mess, oh my!
I search for the Big Dipper, but I can't say why.
The North Star has taken a break, it seems,
While comets play hide and seek in my dreams.

Galaxies twirl in curious dances,
As I trip over my own circumstances.
Jupiter's lost his sparkly crown,
And Saturn's rings are upside down!

The sun shines bright, but it's hard to see,
When planets forget how to play properly.
Asteroids trip and fall on the ground,
Creating a show that's quite profound.

I thought I could map out the whole night sky,
But it seems I'm just chasing a twinkling lie.
With stardust in my hair and moonbeams in tow,
I laugh at the chaos, letting it flow.

The Canvases We Leave Behind

In the art of living, I dropped my brush,
Splashing colors that create a rush.
The canvas is splotchy, a chaotic spree,
With fingerprints where my thoughts used to be.

Each stroke tells a story, but it's muddled for sure,
A Picasso of plans, can I endure?
With laughter and giggles splattered around,
I create a masterpiece that won't be found.

My palette is wild, a carnival mix,
In the gallery of blunders, I get my kicks.
The paint's still drying, and I just can't wait,
For the next twist in fate, which I can't anticipate.

I might not be Van Gogh or the wise old Rembrandt,
But my masterpiece winks, oh isn't it grand?
For in each vibrant hue, unfolds a sigh,
As I dance in the chaos, beneath the sky.

Steps on the Frayed Path

Wandering down this quirky old lane,
Where logic takes breaks, and sanity's slain.
The signs are all crooked, the map's upside down,
While squirrels throw nuts like they're holding a crown.

Each step's like a jig, a chuckle or two,
As I skip through the thorns just to needle a view.
Why follow the straight when the crooked's in play?
I'm carving my journey, come join the ballet!

The footprints are shifting, a dance with no lead,
As I tumble and giggle, what a fine steed!
With flower pots falling and laughter at hand,
Every misstep's a party, oh isn't it grand?

So I'll shuffle along with my toes in the grass,
In this frayed little path, as I carelessly pass.
Life's a wild groove, let's sway and not fret,
For the joy of the journey's my favorite duet!

Regions of Disarray

In a land where the socks go to hide,
And breakfast cereal dances with pride.
My keys play a game of runaway tag,
As my coffee pot's staging a messy old brag.

The fridge speaks in riddles, it's a curious sight,
With leftovers plotting to take wing at night.
I open its door, what chaos unfurls,
Like a sitcom stage, with food in swirls.

Each corner's a riddle, a twist of the fate,
My calendar's scribbles, a jumbled state.
Yet in every miscue, I find a delight,
Laughing at mishaps that feel just right!

So here in the mess, I twirl and I spin,
In this wacky old loop, let the fun times begin!
For in regions of disarray, I see oh so clear,
That a life full of giggles is the best souvenir!

www.ingramcontent.com/pod-product-compliance
Lightning Source LLC
Chambersburg PA
CBHW051643160426
43209CB00004B/776